TROLLS

Raintree is an imprint of Capstone Global Library Limited, a company incorporated in England and Wales having its registered office at 264 Banbury Road, Oxford, OX2 7DY – Registered company number: 6695582

www.raintree.co.uk
myorders@raintree.co.uk

Hardback edition © Capstone Global Library Limited 2022
Paperback edition © Capstone Global Library Limited 2023
The moral rights of the proprietor have been asserted.

All rights reserved. No part of this publication may be reproduced in any form or by any means (including photocopying or storing it in any medium by electronic means and whether or not transiently or incidentally to some other use of this publication) without the written permission of the copyright owner, except in accordance with the provisions of the Copyright, Designs and Patents Act 1988 or under the terms of a licence issued by the Copyright Licensing Agency, 5th Floor, Shackleton House, 4 Battle Bridge Lane, London SE1 2HX (www.cla.co.uk). Applications for the copyright owner's written permission should be addressed to the publisher.

Editor: Julie Gassman
Designer: Hilary Wacholz

Original illustrations © Capstone Global Library Limited 2020
Originated by Capstone Global Library Ltd

ISBN 978 1 3982 3515 1 (hardback)
ISBN 978 1 3982 3516 8 (paperback)

British Library Cataloguing in Publication Data
A full catalogue record for this book is available from the British Library.

All the internet addresses (URLs) given in this book were valid at the time of going to press. However, due to the dynamic nature of the internet, some addresses may have changed, or sites may have changed or ceased to exist since publication. While the author and publisher regret any inconvenience this may cause readers, no responsibility for any such changes can be accepted by either the author or the publisher.

Printed and bound in India.

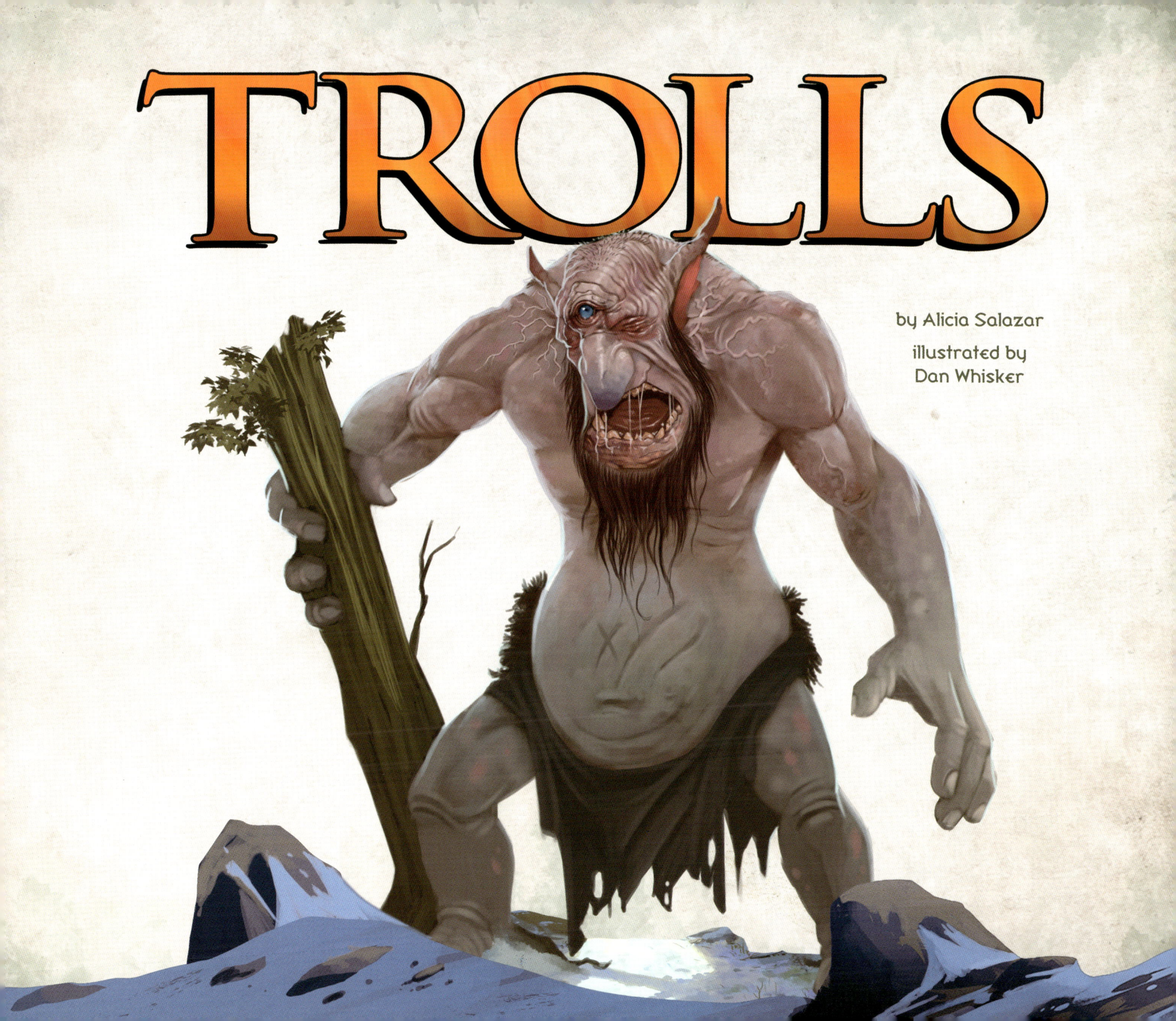

TROLLS

by Alicia Salazar

illustrated by Dan Whisker

Deep in a forest, a troll hides under a bridge. He is huge. He looks like he is made of stone. The troll has a single eye. He waits for a human to approach.

He will stop anyone who dares to cross the bridge. He gives them one chance to solve a riddle. If they solve it, they may pass. If they don't, he will eat them!

TROLL BEHAVIOUR

Trolls are mythical creatures. They are known for being unfriendly towards humans. Early stories about trolls came from Scandinavia more than 3,000 years ago. In these stories, trolls were giant monsters. Few people had seen them.

According to legends, trolls like to stay in the shadows. They usually only come out after the sun goes down. If they are caught in sunlight, they will turn to stone.

Trolls are wealthy. They have mountains of coins and jewels hidden away. No one knows where they get their riches from.

Humans have often tried to take their riches. They have tried to outsmart trolls. Few people have succeeded. Most have ended up as the troll's dinner.

Most trolls kidnap and eat humans. Since trolls are made of stone, they are very strong. Giant trolls can rip trees out of the ground. They use them to hit humans. Trolls are magical. They cast spells that can control human behaviour.

There are few defences against trolls. But the sound of church bells sends them running. They can also be killed with a lightning bolt.

The best way to defeat a troll is by tricking him. Most trolls are not very clever. A human can gain a troll's treasure by outsmarting him.

Giant trolls live alone, but smaller trolls live in communities with other trolls. Their homes are faraway caves, rocks or mountains. Only a few stolen objects decorate the homes. Most have a fireplace for cooking and furs for warmth.

Some trolls can shape-shift. They can make themselves look like humans in order to trick people. Trolls who shape-shift might live among humans for days or weeks at a time.

LIFE CYCLE OF A TROLL

All trolls are born from stone. No one knows exactly how. Some say they walk out of a rock fully grown. Others say they go through all the stages humans go through: infant, child, teenager, adult.

Several legends tell of trolls that kidnap human babies. They replace the humans with troll babies. The troll babies are called changelings. They grow up looking just like a human. But they have the minds and abilities of trolls.

TYPES OF TROLLS

All trolls are originally from Scandinavia. But not all trolls look alike. Mountain and forest trolls are gigantic, smelly and scary looking. Their arms and legs look like stone. Some have more than one head or only one eye.

MOUNTAIN TROLL

Cave trolls are smaller than humans. They live underground and have round bellies and short arms. But they are just as ugly as mountain trolls.

CAVE TROLL

LITTLE FOLK

According to legend, there is also a group of small trolls called the little folk. They can often pass for humans as long as they hide their tails.

HEAD OR HEADS
Trolls can have two, three or even eight large heads.

EYE OR EYES
Many trolls are cyclopes. They have only one eye. But most have two.

ARMS AND LEGS
Trolls' arms and legs are usually large and hard like rock.

HAIR
Trolls live in the wild and rarely brush their hair. Their hair is messy and tangled. It might even have a bird's nest in it.

BODY
Plants often grow from soil trapped in the rocky cracks of trolls' bodies.

TROLLS OF MYTH

The most famous legend about trolls is the story of the Three Billy Goats Gruff. In the story, three billy goats want to cross a bridge to reach a meadow. A troll tries to stop them from crossing. He threatens to eat them. In the end, the billy goats trick him and get away.

Another legend tells the story of a young girl who was kidnapped by trolls. They took her into the mountains. She cried and cried until the trolls grew tired of her and let her go. Before they sent her back, one troll hit her with a club. As a result, she was hunchbacked for the rest of her life.

Another story is about a helpful troll. A man called Lars rode a horse past an injured troll woman in a ditch. She called out to him. At first, he ignored her and moved on. Still, he kept hearing a voice asking for help.

Finally, he went back. Lars gave the troll the help she needed. In return, she helped him magically be on time for everything for the rest of his life.

Troll legends are most common in Norway and Iceland. In Norway, people can even visit places called Troll's Tongue and Troll's Ladder.

But trolls can be found everywhere. Look closely when you are walking in a forest or near mountains or caves. You might meet a troll with a riddle for you. If you keep your wits about you, you could end up with some treasure!

ABOUT THE AUTHOR

Alicia Salazar is a Mexican American children's book author who has written for blogs, magazines and education publishers. She has been a school teacher and a marine biologist. She currently lives on the outskirts of Houston, Texas, USA, but is a city girl at heart. When she is not dreaming up new adventures to experience, she is turning her adventures into stories for children.

ABOUT THE ILLUSTRATOR

Dan Whisker is a self-taught illustrator who previously enjoyed careers in the military and then the police force. Dan is married with three grown-up children and currently lives in a small village near Canterbury.

GLOSSARY

ability skill

changeling child secretly switched for another as a baby

community group of creatures that live in the same area

hunchbacked having a humped or crooked back

legend story passed down through the years that may not be completely true

mythical based on stories from ancient times

Scandinavia part of northern Europe that includes Norway, Denmark and Sweden

shape-shift change form or appearance

wits ability to think and act clearly

COMPREHENSION QUESTIONS

1. You have probably seen films or read other stories about trolls. Compare the trolls from those to the trolls this book talks about. How are they the same? How are they different?

2. Thinking about what you've read, would you want to meet a troll? Explain your answer.

3. Create your own troll. Draw a picture of your troll and write a description, including how the troll sounds and smells.

FIND OUT MORE

BOOKS

Discover Dragons, Giants and Other Deadly Fantasy Monsters, Aaron J. Sautter (Raintree, 2017)

Listen, My Bridge Is So Cool! The Story of the Three Billy Goats Gruff as Told by the Troll, Nancy Loewen (Raintree, 2018)

Myths, Legends and Sacred Stories: A Children's Encyclopedia, DK (DK Children, 2019)

WEBSITE

The Mythology of Norwegian Trolls
lifeinnorway.net/norwegian-trolls

READ THEM ALL!

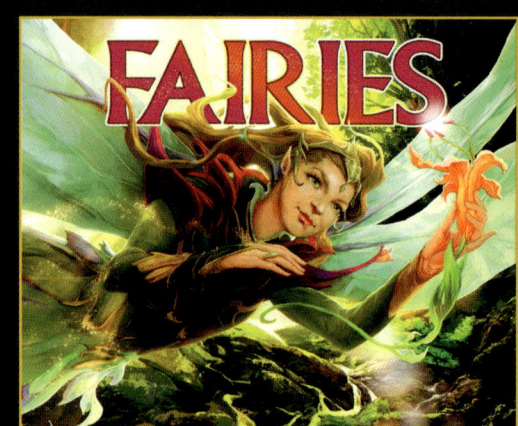

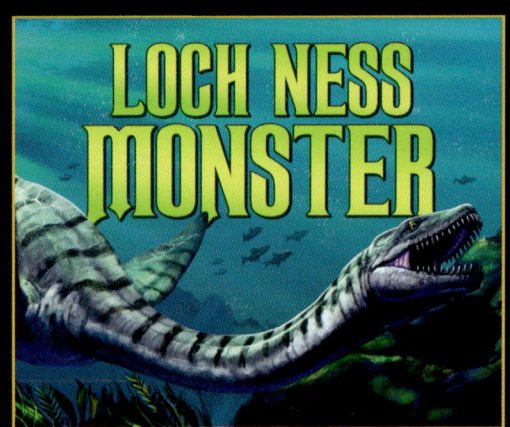
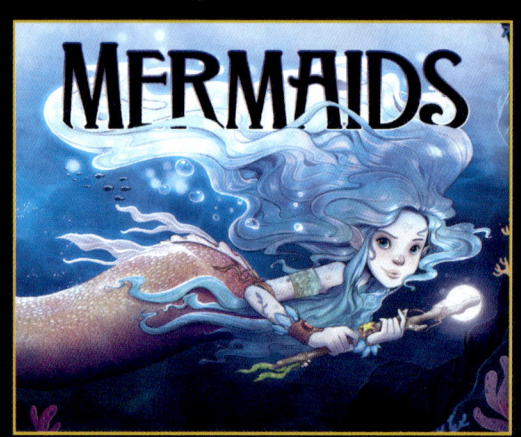